**JAMIE
KYLE
MCGILLIAN**

STERLING CHILDREN'S BOOKS
New York

To Bailey Ann and Devan Brooke,
who always bring the questions, the love, and the laughs.
To Geno, who brings the answers.

STERLING CHILDREN'S BOOKS
New York

An Imprint of Sterling Publishing Co., Inc.
1166 Avenue of the Americas
New York, NY 10036

ISBN 978-1-4549-2336-7

Library of Congress Cataloging-in-Publication Data

Names: McGillian, Jamie Kyle, author.
Title: Quiz me! / Jamie Kyle McGillian.
Description: New York, NY : Sterling Children's Books, 2017.
Identifiers: LCCN 2016048524 | ISBN 9781454923367 (paperback)
Subjects: LCSH: Identity (Psychology)--Juvenile literature. | Children's
  questions and answers. | BISAC: JUVENILE NONFICTION / Games &
  Activities / Questions & Answers. | JUVENILE NONFICTION / Activity
  Books. | JUVENILE NONFICTION / Games & Activities / General.
Classification: LCC BF697 .M224 2017 | DDC 155.2--dc23 LC record available
at https://lccn.loc.gov/2016048524

Distributed in Canada by Sterling Publishing Co., Inc.
c/o Canadian Manda Group, 664 Annette Street
Toronto, Ontario, Canada M6S 2C8
Distributed in the United Kingdom by GMC Distribution Services
Castle Place, 166 High Street, Lewes, East Sussex, England BN7 1XU
Distributed in Australia by NewSouth Books
45 Beach Street, Coogee, NSW 2034, Australia

For information about custom editions, special sales, and premium and
corporate purchases, please contact Sterling Special Sales at 800-805-5489
or specialsales@sterlingpublishing.com.

Manufactured in Canada

Lot :
2   4   6   8   10   9   7   5   3   1
06/17

www.sterlingpublishing.com

Line art by Bethany Robertson
Title page photo © Juan Monino/iStockphoto (girl)
Design by Ryan Thomann

CONTENTS

INTRODUCTION

Have you ever wondered what animal you are most like? Or what your superpower would be if you had one? Get ready to find out! This book is full of quizzes to help you think about everything from what season is your best season, to which hairstyle best suits your personality, to which book character you are most like. It's all fun and games, but quizzes do help us learn about ourselves. If you have ever wondered "Who am I really?" and "Who do I want to be?" this is the book for you!

HOW TO USE THIS BOOK

People of all ages can use the quizzes in this book to ask and answer questions and then share their results. The quizzes are also fun to take on your own. When you do them with a bunch of friends, you can each write down your answers on separate pieces of paper or take pictures of the pages with your phones and type in your answers in your Notes app. After you answer for yourself, answer for your friend and see how well you know her.

You might find yourself knee-deep in a quiz where the responses just don't quite fit your personality. That's okay. The trick is to figure out the choice that is most like you. Sometimes it will be a perfect fit. Other times, it won't.

Take this question:

5. If you feel like being adventurous, you might

    a. put sliced strawberries on your frozen yogurt.

    b. jump off the high diving board at the pool.

    c. take a shortcut to school.

    d. volunteer to be the first person in your class to get a flu shot.

You might be leaning toward choice **a**, but you might be allergic to strawberries, or you may just not like them. It's still all right to answer **a**. It is understood that **a** would be your best choice if you were not allergic to strawberries or if you liked them.

Above all, the important thing is to have fun while you take these quizzes. Laughing is definitely encouraged!

Post your results on your favorite social media site or just share them with your best buds. Are you ready to get your quiz on?

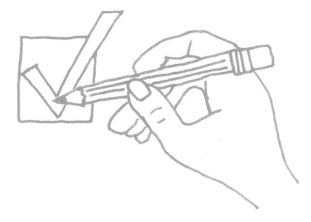

Maddie

QUIZ 1

What do you think makes you a good friend? Are you someone who always listens and can easily calm a friend in need? Or do you make everyone laugh in both good times and bad times? **Let's find out.**

1. **A good friend is someone who**
    a. always knows what to do.
    b. cares about my feelings.
    c. can make me laugh so hard that I snort.
    d. thinks I rule the world.

2. **How would you and your besties celebrate National Best Friend Day?**
    a. With homemade smoothies and a poem about friendship
    b. With a group hug and a photo shoot
    c. With matching T-shirts that read "Happy National Best Friend Day"
    d. With a trip to the butterfly exhibit at the zoo

3. **Your friend just told you a big, juicy secret. What will you do?**
    a. Keep it to myself—it's the right thing to do
    b. Wait, what secret?
    c. Joke about how the secret is dying to come out
    d. Tell someone who doesn't know the person what the secret is about

4. What do you love to do most with your friends?

    a. Play games or go on hikes

    b. Sit around and talk

    c. Watch funny movies

    d. Turn the music up and dance

5. What do you and your friends usually chat about?

    a. Silly things that happen at school or things we're learning about

    b. How we're feeling that day

    c. Inside jokes

    d. What happened in the hallway with my crush that morning

6. What's your favorite way to spend an afternoon?

    a. By myself doing homework or yoga

    b. Having lunch at a new pizza place with a pal

    c. In a big group, laughing and acting silly

    d. Outside in a hot air balloon (or at least on a bike)

7. If your best friend just started hanging out with someone you are not friends with, what would you do?

    a. Start by saying hello to the new person

    b. Talk to my friend about how we are both feeling

    c. Joke about how the new person is taking my place

    d. Have a party to welcome the new person into our friend group

8. What interests you most?

    a. A fun science experiment or a tricky math problem

    b. A good book

    c. The latest celebrity gossip and tweets

    d. Fashion, sports, space travel

Pat

9. If your friend is upset, you would suggest that she
   a. go for a walk or a run to clear her head.
   b. talk to you about her feelings.
   c. see a funny movie with a bunch of friends.
   d. check out the new skate park in town to take her mind off it.

10. Your friendship style can be compared to
   a. a battery: it just keeps on going.
   b. a convenience store: open all the time with all the things a person needs.
   c. an open book: it makes for a great story.
   d. a party: full of excitement and energy.

11. When you are with your group of friends, you feel
   a. relaxed and comfortable.
   b. warm and open.
   c. like the center of attention.
   d. like you can do anything.

12. You have plans to meet friends at the park. Your good friend calls to say she can't go because her grandmother is ill. You

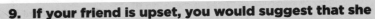

   a. come up with something the two of you can do to take her mind off it.
   b. offer to keep her company while she waits for news.
   c. go to the park but try to cheer her up with hourly texts.
   d. drop off a new comic book for her on your way to the park.

13. You know that if you want a good friend, you have to be a good friend. That's why you

    a. talk to your friend about everything, from friends, to family, to dreams.

    b. try to think of a solution whenever your friend has a problem.

    c. know the best ways to make her laugh.

    d. invite her to the zoo, to paintball, and to the beach.

14. You love your best friend so much, you would

    a. stand up for her if another friend put her down.

    b. share your French fries with her.

    c. take her on vacation with you.

    d. give her all of your French fries because you know how much she loves them.

15. For Valentine's Day, your crush sends you a chocolate heart, but your best friend hasn't gotten anything. What do you do?

    a. Mention it once and then don't bring it up again unless she does

    b. Share my chocolate and give her a goofy homemade Valentine

    c. Give her a bunch of heart stickers and tell her how much I care about her

    d. Go out and get manicures with her

SCORECARD

Keep in mind that it is possible to be more than one type of friend. You can be a joker sometimes but still be wise.

Mostly A's: The Wise One You are an old soul and most likely are headed for a career helping people, because you give really smart and practical advice. A bestie walks up to you and says, "Help, I don't know what to do!" A few minutes later, that friend is thanking you for knowing exactly what to do!

Mostly B's: The Listener You are a true friend who really listens—not just when a friend is hurting but all the time. You have great healing powers. Friends count on you because they know you pay attention to the details and care about them.

Mostly C's: The Joker Ha, ha! You like to laugh and make all your friends laugh. You believe that humor is the best medicine and you know how to spread it around. Your friends are grateful to you for being cheerful in good times and bad. Keep on LOLing!

Mostly D's: The Adventurous One You are not scared of anything, and you try to live life to the fullest. You like to encourage all your friends to take healthy risks—to try out for the team or the play, or to talk to the crush. You're a fun friend to be around!

TAKE ACTION

For one day, try to be an even friendlier version of yourself. Say hello to everyone you know and give people extra smiles when you want to. At the end of the day, think about how effective your friendly behavior was. Did people treat you differently? Were your smiles returned?

QUIZ 2

Maddie

WHAT'S YOUR PERSONAL STYLE?

What you wear can say a lot about who you are. Do you follow the trends, or could you care less about wearing the latest designer clothes? Does your style best fit the scene at a music festival or at the gym? **Let's find out.**

1. Your earrings right now are
    a. small pink stones.
    b. silver hoops that go with everything.
    c. tiny gold studs.
    d. large, dangling, colorful, and glittery.
    e. in a drawer.

2. Your idea of makeup might be
    a. a dash of mascara and a touch of lip gloss.
    b. dark eye shadow with dark lips.
    c. scented lip gloss.
    d. pink lips, pink cheeks, and dramatic eyes.
    e. clear lip balm.

3. Your perfect amount of jewelry is
    a. four or five trendy bracelets and a small gold heart necklace.
    b. a large crystal pendant necklace, leather cuffs, beaded bracelets—the more the merrier.
    c. a small ring and a delicate gold chain necklace.
    d. lots of big clunky costume jewelry.
    e. a mood ring.

4. Your ultimate bedspread would be

   a. pink and white daisies . . . with matching pillows.

   b. black and gray swirls with hints of purple.

   c. a solid navy-blue comforter with white pillows.

   d. pink satin with a half dozen small cream-colored lace pillows.

   e. whatever is on my bed.

5. A favorite Saturday afternoon outfit might be

   a. a flouncy skirt, a pink-and-white striped top, and strappy sandals.

   b. dark skinny jeans, a vintage concert T-shirt, and short black boots.

   c. black yoga pants, a matching warm-up sweatshirt, and white sneakers.

   d. a white lace maxidress, red belt, black cowboy boots, and short jean jacket.

   e. jeans and a T-shirt and your favorite old sneakers.

6. At the beach, you

   a. swim a bit, lie on your blanket for a while (with a fresh coat of sunblock, of course), then plan a sleepover bash with friends.

   b. visit the local farmers market on the way there and then enjoy fresh snacks while reading up on the latest local bands.

   c. run along the water, eat some watermelon, then go for a swim.

   d. take selfies with your buds in your cute cover-ups, then play loud music and turn the scene into a party.

   e. swim, make a sand castle, snack on chips, and collect shells.

7. What's most important to you?

a. Looking and feeling my very best

b. Trying new foods, going to secondhand stores for fashion tips, talking about pop culture

c. Being active, doing well in sports, being with my friends

d. Summer concerts, taking old pieces of clothes and mixing with new pieces

e. Family, friends, looking forward to parties and celebrations

8. What does your favorite shirt look like?

a. It has a designer label.

b. It's black with a funny message: "Don't eat yellow snow!"

c It has a Nike logo.

d. It's got flowing sleeves.

e. It might have a tiny pizza stain on it from last week.

9. Chances are, your nails are

a. manicured and polished pink.

b. short and polished black.

c. neatly filed with a clear coat of polish.

d. polished in a neon color.

e. clean (maybe).

10. If you were to get a temporary tattoo, it might be of a

a. sailboat.

b. winding road with the words "Keep on truckin'."

c. moon and stars.

d. a few music notes.

e a happy face.

11. A thin bracelet around your wrist might read

    a. "LOVE."

    b. "There's a song in my heart."

    c. "Refuse to Lose!"

    d. "True Friends."

    e. "Mom."

12. For lunch, you might enjoy

    a. a salad with grilled chicken.

    b. artichoke hummus and pita bread.

    c. pasta with broccoli.

    d. a hot pretzel and a bagel with cream cheese.

    e. a peanut butter and jelly sandwich.

13. Where do you get your fashion ideas?

    a. From fashion magazines

    b. By looking at what everyone is wearing

    c. On the field

    d. Combining old and new pieces to create original looks

    e. What fashion ideas?

14. When you think about a prom, what do you imagine yourself wearing?

    a. A pink frilly gown with sequins and heels

    b. A black dress with red boots and a black leather jacket

    c. A navy-blue cotton dress with white sandals

    d. A long, strappy, gauzy maxidress with a pink scarf and strappy sandals

    e. Something pretty

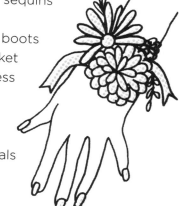

15. Which is an accessory that just would not work for you?

a. A black fedora

b. A white canvas tote

c. Long, dangly earrings

d. A sporty tennis skirt

e. A fur shawl

16. Your favorite fragrance might be

a. floral.

b. musky.

c. clean with a hint of cinnamon.

d. a mix of coconut and vanilla.

e. uh, chocolate?

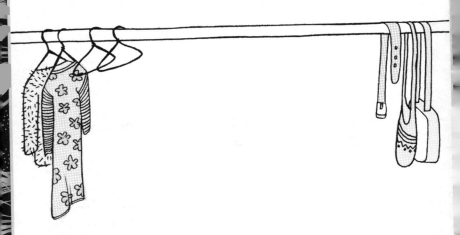

SCORECARD

Mostly A's: Girly-Girl You love looking your best, and to you that means looking feminine at all times. You wear form-fitting jeans, flouncy skirts, and baby doll dresses with spaghetti straps. Girly jewelry, nail polish, and a nice shoulder bag complement your look. You like romance and favor upbeat music. Your idea of fun on a Saturday night is dressing up with all your gal pals.

Mostly B's: Hipster You are intellectual and crazy about pop culture and music. When you grow up, you want to travel. You are very interested in politics and the environment. You love shopping at secondhand stores. One of your favorite looks is skinny jeans and an oversized flannel plaid shirt with black boots. You think it could be fun to dye your hair blue or hot pink—maybe you already have!

Mostly C's: Sports Star You love to kick it on the soccer field or the tennis courts. Playing and talking about sports is one of your favorite things to do, and you're very close to your teammates. In terms of clothes, you like simple things that are well made: athletic apparel, sweat suits, tennis gear, T-shirts, sports caps, and baggy basketball shorts. You keep your hair nice and neat in a ponytail.

Mostly D's: Festival Chic

This look is also called the Coachella or Bohemian look. You love being outdoors, listening to music, and celebrating your unique style. At summer concerts, you show up in wide-bottom pants and delicate tops; frilly, gauzy fabrics are your faves. You like a dash of sequins here and there, and you love long jewelry that is artistic and colorful. Try finding a wide-brim hat you like—they're fun to throw on with almost any outfit.

Mostly E's: Style Factor Undecided

You're not always sure what you like to wear, and that is totally fine! Enjoy not being a slave to fashion and wear anything you want—jeans, dresses, jumpers, blouses, jean jackets, T-shirts. Love the outfit and love yourself in it. You can even feel free to invent your own look! Try any of these fun ideas: a fedora, a cat-print pocketbook, tie-dyed shirts, pretty pastel-colored camisoles under your shirts, or temporary tattoos. Experiment with all kinds of looks.

TAKE ACTION

Widen your style by looking at pieces from other styles and incorporating them into your wardrobe. Set up a clothing and accessories swap with friends to add some fresh looks to your closet without breaking the bank!

QUIZ 3

It was a day like any other. You were walking down the street. You had your books in one hand and a water bottle in the other. All of a sudden, everything changed. Cool in every sense of the word, just the sight of this person made you feel that your heart was going to burst out of your chest. When that person's eyes met yours, you felt a certain magnetic charge . . . or something like that. It was so powerful. From that second, you felt like you needed to talk to that person. *Who is this person who makes me act like this?* you wondered. It's your very first crush, and it's crazy, mad, intense. How intense? Let's find out.

1. When you get dressed in the morning, what are you thinking about?

a. One of my many crushes

b. How to make sure my crush is my science partner today

c. Going back to bed

d. Mostly my upcoming math test, but thinking about a certain person makes me smile

2. **When you close your eyes and think of your happy place, what do you see?**

   a. My cozy room

   b. The skate park, full of all my friends

   c. A spinach and mushroom pizza waiting for me and my crush to dive into

   d. Me and my crush on the Ferris wheel

3. **When you are around your crush, you find yourself**

   a. acting shy.

   b. acting normal.

   c. acting weird.

   d. a and c.

4. **Do you find yourself going places where your crush is known to hang out?**

   a. No. If I did, my crush might suspect.

   b. I want to go, but I don't dare.

   c. Um, yes.

   d. No. I don't think I'd have fun there.

5. **If a friend said something not so great about your crush, you would**

   a. ignore it.

   b. question the crush.

   c. be insulted.

   d. question the friendship.

6. **Sometimes you are so wrapped up in thoughts about your crush that you**

   a. forget to text your friend back.

   b. laugh at your own silliness because this is a side of you that no one ever sees.

   c. imagine the two of you on your wedding day.

   d. don't hear your teacher calling on you.

7. If you see your crush talking to someone else, you may

  a. post a selfie and do whatever it takes to get your crush to see it.
  b. feel a bit jealous.
  c. yell "Fire" to break them apart.
  d. pretend not to care.

8. Who knows about your crush?

  a. My whole extended family
  b. Me and my mom
  c. Me and my diary
  d. Basically everyone except for my crush—I hope!

9. Let's say you hated sushi. What if that was your crush's favorite food?

  a. Um, I still don't think I could eat it.
  b. I'd order a California roll pronto.
  c. I'd give it a try.
  d. I'd eat sushi for breakfast, lunch, and dinner.

10. What would you do if your crush showed up at your front door?

  a. I'd try to act natural.
  b. I'd probably faint.
  c. I'd run for the back door.
  d. I'd invite him in.

11. What if your friend had a crush on your crush?

  a. Great! We could talk about how cute our crush is together.
  b. I would try to tone down my feelings for the crush.
  c. I would fight to win the affections of my crush even if it cost me my friendship.
  d. I'd be crushed.

12. Each time someone mentions your crush's name, you

  a. tune out everything else.

  b. share a giggle with your friend.

  c. can't help but smile.

  d. blush.

13. Your crush calls you just as you sit down to do homework. You say,

  a. "I've got a ton of homework to do. Can I call you back later?"

  b. "Do you want to go over the Spanish vocab words?"

  c. "Can you come over right now?"

  d. "Will you marry me?"

14. The night of your best friend's birthday party, your crush asks you to hang out. You

  a. ask for a rain check. Your crush will understand.

  b. tell your crush it's a date. Then buy your best friend a very generous birthday gift.

  c. invite your crush to the party and hope your best friend will forgive you.

  d. stay in that night and don't bother with the crush or the party.

SCORECARD

Go over your answers and give yourself points according to the following chart:

1. a = 1, b = 3, c = 0, d = 2
2. a = 0, b = 1, c = 2, d = 3
3. a = 2, b = 0, c = 1, d = 3
4. a = 2, b = 1, c = 3, d = 0
5. a = 1, b = 0, c = 2, d = 3
6. a = 2, b = 0, c = 3, d = 1
7. a = 3, b = 1, c = 2, d = 0

8. a = 2, b = 1, c = 0, d = 3
9. a = 0, b = 2, c = 1, d = 3
10. a = 0, b = 3, c = 2, d = 1
11. a = 1, b = 0, c = 3, d = 2
12. a = 3, b = 2, c = 0, d = 1
13. a = 0, b = 1, c = 2, d = 3
14. a = 0, b = 3, c = 2, d = 1

0–14 Points: Crush Factor Mostly in Check

You may be beginning to take notice of someone, but you're not really changing your behavior in any way. That's great! Having a crush can be fun, but it shouldn't get in the way of your schoolwork or time with your friends or family. Still, it's okay to let yourself get a little giggly sometimes.

15–28 Points: Crushing It!

Someone has caught your eye, and you find yourself unable to concentrate. You may be experiencing a slight crush. You may or may not be experiencing a flutter in your chest. Try to keep your cool! Definitely talk to your friends about your crush and listen when they talk about theirs—you can help sort out one another's feelings!

29–42 Points: Crazy with the Crush! Everywhere you look, you see your crush. Every one of your thoughts has something to do with your crush. Try not to go overboard. Just remember that in most cases, a crush stays a crush. It's rare that these feelings develop into a lasting relationship. Have fun and remember—someone else might be crushing on you!

TAKE ACTION

If you have ever wondered if you are spending too much time thinking about your crush, don't worry. Lisa Tager is a Massachusetts-based psychotherapist who works with children and teens. She helps young people deal with problems. Tager says it's important to have crushes. She says having a crush is "a way to test out feelings related to intimacy and caring. It's kind of like a rehearsal for that romantic relationship that you will one day have." So when does a crush become a problem? Tager says, "If thinking about the crush is getting in the way of everyday life—time with friends, homework, school life—you should definitely talk with parents and/or a guidance counselor to help you put the crush in perspective." The important thing about a crush is to keep it relaxed and have fun with it.

QUIZ 4

Are you always thinking about ways to preserve and protect our planet? We can all afford to reduce our carbon footprint—some of us more than others. That may mean using less energy or recycling more. Are you on the right path toward keeping things green? Let's find out.

1. **What are you sure to shut off when brushing your teeth?**
   a. The water faucet
   b. My music
   c. My mind
   d. All of the above

2. **How long does a typical shower last for you?**
   a. It can last the whole morning.
   b. Not more than thirty minutes.
   c. I don't shower unless I have to.
   d. Not more than five minutes.

3. **As you leave a room, you usually**
   a. smile and say "Peace out!" to your parents
   b. make sure to leave a light on so that you're not scared when you get home.
   c. shut off the air conditioner.
   d. shut the lights off, of course.

4. Before leaving for school, you

    a. usually straighten your hair—and sometimes leave your charger plugged in.

    b. make sure to unplug chargers and appliances.

    c. take a long shower, wash your face twice, curl your hair, then decide it looks bad and straighten it.

    (d.) shut your bedroom door to preserve cool air from the air conditioner.

5. What must you never forget when going to the grocery store?

    a. Your paper shopping list

    b. Your shopping list on your phone

    c. Money

    (d.) Reusable bags to carry the groceries

6. One of your favorite activities is to

    a. go on a hike.

    b. plant trees and flowers.

    c. make your own greeting cards and stationery from recycled paper.

    (d.) prank call all the boys you know.

7. Your toilet paper is

    a. the cheapest brand, and I try not to use too much.

    b. I've never examined it closely.

    (c.) extra-soft.

    d. made from 100 percent recycled material.

8. You make your own lunch and carry it in a

    a. reusable lunch pack.

    b. Wait a minute, I buy my lunch.

    c. plastic bag.

    d. brown paper bag with your name on it. How cute!

9. Your idea of a great time is to hang out with friends at

    a. someone's house, watching a movie.

    b. a coffee shop, playing on your phones.

    c. school, for a meeting of the environmental club.

    d. a local park.

10. Your motto is

    a Life is short. Treat yourself!

    b. Drink lots of water.

    c. Clean your plate because leftovers are a big waste of food.

    d. Reduce, reuse, recycle.

11. Something that is really important to you is

    a. walking, biking, or taking public transportation whenever possible.

    b. my phone.

    c. playing outside every day.

    d. treating my siblings nicely.

12. A great way to save water is to

    a. reuse your bathwater.

    b. invest in a huge water cooler.

    c. buy more bottled water and use it to make your own tea.

    d. collect rainwater in a pail and use it to feed the plants.

13. When it comes to lunch, you like to

    a. eat junk food.

    b. make a meal with fresh ingredients from your garden.

    c. eat a burger or a salad at the local coffee shop.

    d. order a pizza to be delivered.

14. You like to celebrate Earth Day by

    a. baking Earth Day cupcakes for all.

    b. buying a cute Earth Day outfit.

    c. Earth Day? That's a day?

    d. spreading the word about ways to care for the planet.

15. An fun idea for a friend's birthday gift might be a

    a. safe, stainless-steel water bottle.

    b. recycle bin.

    c. bag of your used clothing.

    d. cute puppy.

16. One day, you just might

    a buy food only from local farmers.

    b. walk on the moon.

    c. learn to windsurf.

    d. develop my own line of green cleaning products that don't harm the environment.

SCORECARD

Go over your answers and give yourself points according to the following chart:

1. a = 2, b = 1, c = 0, d = 3
2. a = 0, b = 1, c = 3, d = 2
3. a = 0, b = 1, c = 2, d = 3
4. a = 1, b = 3, c = 0, d = 2
5. a = 1, b = 2, c = 0, d = 3
6. a = 1, b = 3, c = 2, d = 0
7. a = 2, b = 1, c = 0, d = 3
8. a = 3, b = 2, c = 0, d = 1
9. a = 1, b = 0, c = 3, d = 2
10. a = 0, b = 1, c = 2, d = 3
11. a = 3, b = 0, c = 2, d = 1
12. a = 3, b = 1, c = 0, d = 2
13. a = 0, b = 3, c = 2, d = 1
14. a = 2, b = 1, c = 0, d = 3
15. a = 3, b = 2, c = 1, d = 0
16. a = 2, b = 0, c = 1, d = 3

0-10 Points: Try a Little Green

It's time to open your eyes and start thinking about the environment. Read up on ways to help the earth. Talk about it with friends and family. Ask yourself, "What can I be doing to save energy, to use less garbage, or to help animals live healthier lives?" Work with friends to come up with small changes and big ideas!

11-23 Points: Change It Up for the Green

You don't have to change your whole life to help the planet. But you can make small, simple changes such as unplugging batteries and appliances when nobody is using them, turning off lights when you leave a room, and recycling plastics. Learn the basics and start implementing earth-saving ideas. You can make a difference!

24-37 Points: Let's Go Green

You are well on your way to being green! You understand what's happening to the planet, and you want to get involved. Whatever you are doing, keep doing it, and spread the word.

38-48 Points: Whoa, You Are Green!

Congratulations; you're really thinking about the planet. Earth is not just where you hang your hat. Keep on trying to encourage and help others who don't know what to do to help.

TAKE ACTION

Start an environmental or nature club in your school. Get your friends to join and see all the wonderful things you can do to help take care of the planet.

QUIZ 5

What animal do you most admire? Is there one in particular that reminds you of yourself? For some people, it's obvious. For example, if you are fast and graceful, you might be compared to a cheetah. But it's not always that easy! Which animal are you most like? Let's find out.

1. How athletic would you say you are?
   a. I can climb a tree, do a dance, and then do it again.
   b. I am so athletic that when I run, it looks like I am flying.
   c. I move faster in the water.
   d. I move when I have to.

2. If someone met you for the first time, he might say you are
   a. silly and full of mischief.
   b. graceful and elegant.
   c. smart, playful, and friendly.
   d. a bit on the quiet side.

3. Your favorite way to travel is
   a. by airplane.
   b. on a sleek, superfast train.
   c. riding on a boat.
   d. in a car so that you can stop when you want to.

4. **A bunch of friends stop by to ask if you want to go to the park with them. You**

    a. can't wait to go. Let the giggles begin!
    b. agree to go and immediately launch into a long story so they all pay attention to you.
    c. would rather just stay in and hang with the fam.
    d. say no because you have a date to be with your favorite person—yourself.

5. **If someone asked you to describe yourself in one word, you might say**

    a. curious.
    b. elegant.
    c. gifted.
    d. clever.

6. **Where do you feel happiest?**

    a. Anywhere—as long as I'm with my pals
    b. In the tall grass
    c. In the water, splashing with all my BFFs
    d. Surrounded by family

7. **Your favorite holiday is**

    a. Thanksgiving. Yum!
    b. Fourth of July. Love those fireworks!
    c. Earth Day.
    d. Groundhog Day. Especially if the groundhog sees his shadow.

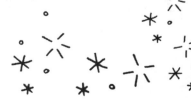

8. **What is your favorite game or activity?**

    a. Musical chairs
    b. Frisbee
    c. Boogie Boarding
    d. Solitaire

9. Who are your closest friends right now?

    a. Basically everyone at school

    b. The same friends I've always had

    c. A small circle of people

    d. My brother/sister (sometimes)

10. What do you do when you get really angry?

    a. I yell and wave my fists in the air.

    b. I stand tall and let off steam.

    c. I breathe and think about what's bothering me.

    d. I release all those not-so-nice thoughts into the air.

11. What's your most delicious lunch?

    a. A big fruit basket would be nice, but really, I will devour whatever is around

    b. A huge salad with lots of stuff

    c. Fresh salmon or tuna

    d. Anything in the fridge—I'm not picky at all

12. How would you describe yourself?

    a. A social butterfly

    b. A dancer

    c. A best friend to all

    d. A dark shadow

13. Which is most important to you?

    a. Phones and other gadgets

    b. My makeup mirror

    c. The local swimming pool

    d. My tree house

14. What advice would your mom give you?

    a. "Don't act too silly with your friends!"

    b. "Always put on a happy face!"

    c. "Don't be afraid to show your true colors!"

    d. "Don't be afraid to open up!"

15. If you have to study for a test, you would most like to do it

    a. with a bunch of friends . . . maybe even your whole class.

    b. with just one partner.

    c. with a study guide in a small, quiet group.

    d. in your pajamas with a snack.

16. Which job sounds like the most fun?

    a. A clown

    b. A fashion model

    c. An animal trainer

    d. A police officer

SCORECARD ✓✓

**Keep in mind that it is possible to be
more than one animal type!**

Mostly A's: Monkey You are fun-loving, just like a monkey!
One minute you are silly, and the next minute you are
caring and very affectionate. You can be a little bit messy,
but you're so lovable that people forgive you easily. You
are entertaining and friendly and always very curious!

Mostly B's: Giraffe You are tall and elegant—and very
athletic! You tend to put a lot of effort into how you look,
but you're beautiful on the inside, too. Before people get to
know you, they may think you're a little snooty, but really,
you're just a little quiet—even though you do like to be the
center of attention when you're among close friends.

Mostly C's: Dolphin Intelligent, playful, and friendly, you
would spend most of your time in the water if you could!
You easily accept new friends into your group and
make them feel welcome. Plus, studies have shown that
dolphins can imitate and memorize human behavior.
That's why they call you smarty-pants!

Mostly D's: Wolf Sometimes you can be wary of others
because you're strong, powerful, and proud. There are
many tales in which you're a quick-witted trickster, and
it's true that you can be sly. You like the comfort of being
with your family, but you also love to be alone. And there's
nothing wrong with that!

TAKE ACTION

Plan a trip to the zoo. If you don't live near one, watch some animal videos. Pay attention to the ways different animals do their thing. You can learn a lot about the world this way!

QUIZ 6

WHICH HAIRSTYLE BEST SUITS YOUR PERSONALITY?

Maybe you've heard that certain hairstyles are best for your face shape. But what do you think about certain hairstyles being best for your personality? Do you like to wear your hair long and flowing or in a neat bun? What does that say about who you are? **Let's find out.**

1. When you go to a party, you want to look

    a. dressed up and pretty.

    b. soft and casual.

    c. nice but a little different.

    d. cute.

2. You and your friends are at a local diner for dinner. You order

    a. soup and salad.

    b. a hot open turkey sandwich.

    c. a veggie burger with mashed potatoes.

    d. chocolate-chip pancakes.

3. If you were a color, you would be

    a. navy.

    b. light blue.

    c. neon green.

    d pink.

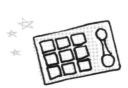

4. At the candy store, you fill your goody bag with

    a. peppermints and a dark chocolate square.

    b. taffy, gumdrops, and jawbreakers.

    c. sugarless gum, chocolate-covered peanuts, and chocolate-covered raisins.

    d. a huge bag of bubble gum.

5. If you could have a mural painted on a wall in your room, it would be a picture of

    a. a city scene.

    b. a horse trotting on the beach.

    c. a horse trotting through a city scene.

    d. you riding on a horse.

6. What would you say is your best facial feature?

    a. Big eyes

    b. Good cheekbones

    c. Nice eyebrows

    d. Full lips

7. If you were a muffin, you would be

    a. blueberry.

    b. corn.

    c. oat bran with raisins.

    d. chocolate chip.

8. For fun, you like to

    a. dress up and take selfies.

    b. shoot hoops with friends.

    c. learn how to read palms.

    d. hit up the local ice cream parlor.

9. Which musician do you like best?

    a. Beyoncé

    b. Taylor Swift

    c. Miley Cyrus

    d. Selena Gomez

10. How would you describe your style?

a. Full of cute, colorful crop-tops

b Casual and comfortable

c. Always mixing it up

d. Lots of dresses and skirts

11. Your best day ever would include

a. lunch with friends and a long shopping session.

b. a sports event that you play in or watch.

c. a trip to an art gallery or museum.

d. going into the fun house at the amusement park. It never gets old!

12. Your favorite finger food is

a. stuffed mushrooms.

b. buffalo wings.

c. mini-pizzas.

d. franks in blankets.

13. If you were a building, you would be

a. a penthouse apartment in a big city.

b. a tiny cottage by a lake.

c. a log cabin deep in the woods.

d. an adorable Tudor house.

14. If you were a shoe, you would be

a. a midcalf clunky black boot.

b. a comfortable sneaker.

c. a furry boot.

d. a Mary Jane.

15. Your favorite weather is

    a. sunny and brisk.

    b. hot and hazy.

    c. cold and rainy.

    d. snowy.

16. If you were a type of soup, you would be

    a. pasta with vegetables.

    b. tomato with rice.

    c. French onion.

    d chicken noodle.

SCORECARD

Mostly A's: Half Up, Half Down You are a person who likes to achieve optimum elegance when putting her hair off her face while letting some strands flow free. Sometimes you love silky, colorful hair wraps because you think they add a little jazz to your classic style. Your hairstyle says that you are confident, smart—and a lot of fun.

Mostly B's: Ponytail You are one sporty gal, and you know what you want and how to get it. A low ponytail suits you fine as you are just coming off the track or running to another club. This cute but practical hairstyle is perfect for your busy lifestyle!

Mostly C's: Braids, Braids, Braids You are intelligent and unique. You wear your hair in braids—on the side, as a crown, in pigtails, whatever!—to express yourself in different ways. Keep rocking your twisty style and try experimenting with French braids and fishtails, too!

Mostly D's: Down with Waves
You like to keep things classic, from your activities to your snacks to your hairstyle. You spend time on your appearance and are put together, but you've definitely got a wild side to you!

TAKE ACTION

Try wearing your hair in a totally new style one day next week. You might be surprised at how nice it is to have it out of your face or how many compliments you get on your pigtail braids!

QUIZ 7

HOW OPTIMISTIC ARE YOU?

The way you view the world can affect your actions and emotions—and vice versa. Do you always look on the bright side? Let's find out.

1. **You are walking down the hallway when someone shoots you a big, bright smile. You**
   a. check to see if you have a stain on your shirt. He was probably laughing at you.
   b. give him a quick grin back and keep walking.
   c. smile back, of course, and ask how his day is going!

2. **Your friend messes up on her oral report about fracking. Afterward, you**
   a. reassure her that she won't get too bad of a grade.
   b. give her a warm smile and point out some positives in her presentation.
   c. make a joke about a part in your presentation that you messed up.

3. **You are smiling**
   a. some of the time.
   b. if someone cracks a joke and it's actually funny.
   c. all the time.

4. **What makes you smile?**
   a. Meeting up with a really good friend
   b. My favorite movies—and I have a lot of them
   c. Funny videos on YouTube

5. **How often do your cry after reading a sad book or watching a sad movie?**

   a. All the time. I love a good cry.

   b. Once in a while if it really moves me.

   c. It depends on how the story ends.

6. **You just got the great news that you've been cast as the lead in the school play! How do you feel?**

   a. Excited but nervous

   b. Worried that halfway through the director will change her mind and cast someone else

   c. Over the moon because this is going to be so fun

7. **You've got a huge decision coming up. You**

   a. trust your gut—it can't be that bad either way, right?

   b. take some time alone to think long and hard about all the possible repercussions.

   c. ask friends and family for their input.

8. **In school, many of your teachers**

   a. ask you to participate more.

   b. don't have much to say about you either way, and you like it like that.

   c. ask you not to raise your hand so often.

9. **On a Monday morning, you are usually**

   a. grumpy. Mondays are rough.

   b. raring to go.

   c. groggy but hopeful that good things will come your way.

10. **When you think about the future of the planet, you are mostly**

   a. hopeful that things will get better.

   b. doubtful that we can turn things around.

   c. worried that things will only get worse.

SCORECARD

Go over your answers and give yourself points according to the following chart:

1. a = 1 b = 2, c = 3
2. a = 1, b = 3, c = 2
3. a = 2, b = 1, c = 3
4. a = 2, b = 3, c = 1
5. a = 3, b = 2, c = 1

6. a = 2, b = 1, c = 3
7. a = 3, b = 1, c = 2
8. a = 1, b = 2, c = 3
9. a = 1, b = 3, c = 2
10. a = 3, b = 2, c = 1

10–16 Points: The Glass Is Half Empty

You lean toward pessimism—you don't often feel confident that everything will turn out all right. It's great to be realistic, and it's normal to worry occasionally, but try to find the silver lining sometimes, too.

17–23 Points: The Glass Is . . . Water?

You like to go with the flow. You are pleasant and happy most of the time, but you do have moments when you seem to frown for no real reason. Keep being yourself, and try to be aware of how your friends' viewpoints may differ from yours.

24–30 Points: The Glass Is Half Full

You are definitely an optimist. To you, the world is full of opportunities—and you're ready to go out there and grab them! Keep in mind that not everyone is always as cheerful as you are. Use your positive attitude to help others, but remember that there may be times when you should tone it down.

TAKE CHARGE

Whether you're a pessimist, an optimist, or in between, there are many health benefits to smiling. It can relax your whole body. Next time you need to cheer up, try smiling!

QUIZ 8

WHAT WOULD YOUR ROLE BE IN A MEDIEVAL KINGDOM?

Medieval times were quite different from today for many reasons. Everyone who was part of the kingdom had a specific role that suited his or her personality. If you lived during that period, what role would you play?

Let's find out.

1. First and foremost, you are
- a. in charge.
- b. brave.
- c. musical.
- d. all about the laughs.

2. On any given Saturday, you are mostly likely to
- a. get your younger siblings to put on a show for you.
- b. go horseback riding at the stables.
- c. write a song and play it for your friends.
- d. crack up your friends with your jokes while you're hanging out at the ice cream parlor.

3. If a snake approached you on a hike, you would
- a. scream for someone to help you.
- b. valiantly toss the snake back into the forest.
- c. calm the snake with your beautiful voice.
- d. be scared but laugh about it afterward.

4. You are really good at

    a. taking the reins on a group project.

    b. fighting for what you believe in.

    c. putting together playlists for parties.

    d. entertaining everyone with your clever wit.

5. Your favorite way to get around is by

    a. horse and buggy.

    b. horseback.

    c. boat.

    d. using your legs.

6. What's your best feature?

    a. My confidence

    b. My strong cheekbones and muscular arms

    c. My vocal chords

    d. My sense of humor

7. Your dream crush is

    a. someone who values family.

    b. brave and daring.

    c. a person who really hears the music.

    d. someone who can see the humor in a serious situation.

8. Rate your love for animals: 1 is not too keen, and 10 is head over heels in love with every animal known to humankind.

    a. 9

    b. 8

    c. 7

    d. 6

9. What is your best subject in school?

a. English. I love talking about books and stories.

b. Social studies. I love hearing stories from history about the brave things people have done.

c. Math and music

d. Science. I like making things explode!

10. For you, music is

a. the soundtrack to your life.

b. inspirational.

c. beautiful and ever-changing, from classic to rap.

d. those silly jingles that you expect to hear while watching cartoons.

11. Your best character traits are

a. your strength and leadership skills.

b. your bravery and loyalty.

c. that you are friendly and not judgmental.

d. that you're a bit rebellious and spirited.

12. The best gift for you would be

a. a town named after you.

b. a collection of swords.

c. a new violin.

d. a collection of books by humorous writers.

SCORECARD

Mostly A's: The Lord or Lady Like the ruler of a kingdom, you like to be in charge. You always try to do what's right for everyone around you. You are well liked, and people want you to like them, too. You have come far and will continue to go places!

Mostly B's: The Knight It was your duty as a Middle Ages knight to learn how to fight and to serve and defend your lord. You did so with extreme bravery. You would have trained many years for knighthood, first as a page and then as a squire. You have a wide variety of skills, but most important, you're brave and adventurous.

Mostly C's: The Minstrel The image of the minstrel is strong. You are first and foremost an entertainer. In your role as minstrel, you sing ballads about love and courage. You are also very smart—minstrels would memorize long texts and recite them to crowds.

Mostly D's: The Jester Jesters were hired to entertain the royal family. They were often the life of the party—just as you often are! If you were lucky enough to be hired by a royal family, you were well respected. Some say you helped the royal family rule with your comments about politics and your clever wit.

TAKE ACTION

Castles, with high stone walls, soundproof rooms, and hidden doors, were built with safety in mind. What would a modern-day castle look like? How would it be safe? How would it be modern? Picture it in your mind and then draw it on paper!

QUIZ 9

WHAT'S YOUR SUPERPOWER?

Calling all superheroes (or would-be superheroes)! If you could have one special ability, what would it be? Can't decide between telepathy and superspeed? Maybe this quiz can help. **Let's find out.**

1. People describe you as
   a. not afraid to pounce.
   b. sharp and ready.
   c. shy; someone who likes to hang back.
   d. fast as lightning.
   e. able to read people.

2. At school, you would be voted
   a. most likely to win a wrestling tournament.
   b. most likely to make a million.
   c. hardest to figure out.
   d. most birdlike.
   e. most likely to solve a crime.

3. Which is your go-to food?
   a. Sautéed spinach
   b. Grilled salmon
   c. I'm not much of an eater.
   d. Anything chocolate
   e. Herbal tea

4. You would want to use your superpowers to rescue someone from

a. a three-headed monster.

b. a huge homework assignment.

c. the school bully.

d. a huge wave.

e. herself.

5. Above all, you are

a. fierce like a tiger.

b. clever like a fox.

c. tricky like a squirrel.

d. fast like a gazelle.

e. all-knowing like an owl.

6. If you lose your house keys, you will get into the house by

a breaking down the door.

b getting in through the side door. It's never locked.

c. slipping through a window.

d. running through town to get the spare set from your mom.

e. finding a hidden extra key somewhere in the yard.

7. You always win at

a. thumb wrestling.

b. chess.

c. hide-and-seek.

d. relay races.

e. Monopoly.

8. What would be your standard superhero outfit?

a. A bodysuit and cape (the cape's really important)

b. An outfit made from state-of-the-art antisweat material

c. Camouflage from head to toe

d. Who cares? Just as long as I have my sneakers!

e. It'd be all black, with reinforced panels at the knees and elbows.

9. Superman had kryptonite as his weakness. Your weakness is your occasional

a. brain freeze.

b. illness.

c. clumsiness.

d. sore muscles.

e. doubts.

10. Do you stand out or blend in?

a. Stand out—a lot

b. Stand out—I tend to answer questions a lot!

c. Blend in—really well

d. Stand out—if people can spot me!

e. Blend in—I keep my mouth shut, even if my mind is busy.

11. While you study, you like to

a. do squats.

b. munch on protein snacks.

c. hole up in your room.

d. put those speed-reading skills to the test!

e. listen to music or have the TV on in the background.

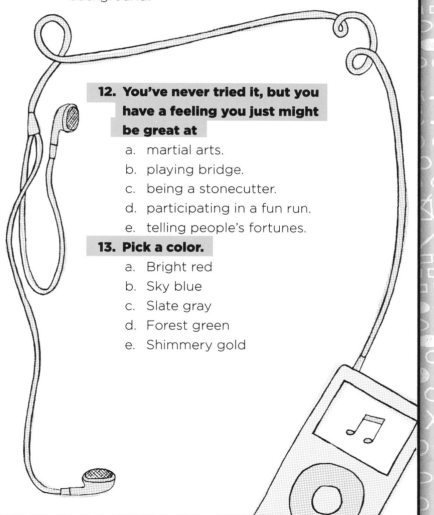

12. You've never tried it, but you have a feeling you just might be great at

a. martial arts.

b. playing bridge.

c. being a stonecutter.

d. participating in a fun run.

e. telling people's fortunes.

13. Pick a color.

a. Bright red

b. Sky blue

c. Slate gray

d. Forest green

e. Shimmery gold

SCORECARD ✓✓

Mostly A's: Superstrength Your physical strength is incredible! You know how to use this power to protect yourself and those around you.

Mostly B's: Mega Brains You are so smart and sharp, you can think your way out of any bad situation. This makes you great at solving problems and a standout member of your superhero squad.

Mostly C's: Invisibility Where are you? I can't see you! Sometimes you are here, sometimes you are there, and sometimes . . . no one knows where you are. While people are wondering where you went off to, you are taking care of business. Being able to be invisible works well for you because you don't like to call attention to yourself.

Mostly D's: Superspeed Wow, look at you running through the city, country, jungle, and mall! You make tracks wherever you go, and you can be relied on to be the fastest hero to get the job done—and outrun whatever supervillain you have to. Just make sure to hydrate!

Mostly E's: Telepathy It's very interesting how you can practically read minds. You are such a good judge of character that you know what those around you are capable of—and you also know things such as what your friend's mom might be making for dinner. How do you do it? You'll never tell.

**Were you close to the limit of one-point range?
Maybe you have multiple superpowers!**

TAKE ACTION

Superpowers may not be real, but it's never too early to sharpen your senses. Try to be more observant when it comes to people and places. Keep a small journal with you at all times and record details, such as what the place or the person looked like and did, in it. Try to include details from all the senses. Do this for a few weeks and you will polish your observation skills. You will be one step closer to becoming a superhero!

HOW INTROVERTED OR EXTROVERTED ARE YOU?

An introvert is a person who prefers being by herself and whose energy level can be drained when she hangs out with others.

An extrovert is a person who is energized when she is with other people. When she is alone, an extrovert can feel bored.

Which do you think you are? Do you come to life in the presence of other people? Or do you like to hang back in a crowd? **Let's find out.**

1. If you are in the class play, you are most likely to be

   a. working on the set.
   b. the star.
   c. designing costumes.
   d. acting in a supporting role.

2. Your teacher says you have a lovely singing voice and wants to put you in the spring recital. You

   a. beg five friends to sing with you so you're not on stage alone.
   b. insist on a solo.
   c. agree happily and practice like crazy.
   d. politely say no. You don't want to be on stage!

3. **For a group science project, you and three classmates have to do a presentation on nutrition. You hope your part will be**

    a. passing out healthful snacks to the audience.

    b. doing most of the talking. How you love a captive audience!

    c. presenting the cool graph you made about how many calories different types of exercise burn— you're really proud of it.

    d. performing the song you made up about the food pyramid.

4. **When a new kid comes to your school, you**

    a. don't say anything to him until you are introduced to him.

    b. walk right up to him and ask him if he'd like to sit with you at lunch.

    c. go up to him with a group of your friends to introduce yourselves.

    d. offer to show him to the math hallway when he looks lost.

5. **When your teacher calls on you to explain how a caterpillar becomes a butterfly,**

    a. you open with a joke to get everyone's attention and then start talking butterflies.

    b. you read aloud the explanation from your textbook.

    c. you look directly at the teacher and share a few facts.

    d. your palms get sweaty and your throat goes dry.

6. **When your best friend's parents ask how your summer vacation was, you**

   a. give them a rundown of the best moments.

   b. answer in one word: "good."

   c. ask for juicy details about their summer vacation

   d immediately take out your phone to share pictures.

7. **You have spent the whole day with friends. In the evening, you**

   a. settle in with one or two pals for pizza and a long chat.

   b. take the time to give your family a running commentary on the day. You make sure not to leave out any details.

   c. are so tired from all those people and all that stimulation that you take an hour to chill before watching a movie with your sibs.

   d. need to unwind in a bath for a long, long time.

8. **You're on a road trip with your friend's family. By the third day, you**

   a. feel like you have bonded with each person in the car.

   b. are drained from having to listening to your friend's father tell the same joke over and over.

   c feel like you need an hour's break from them.

   d. feel like each person in the car is a person you love and trust, and there's so much more to talk about.

9. **When you grow up, the idea of becoming a TV news reporter is**
    a. cool but sounds like it could be exhausting.
    b. an idea that brings waves of nausea and butterflies to your tummy.
    c. is exciting—you've already started practicing your winning smile for the camera.
    d. a definite goal of yours, because you come to life in front of people.

10. **If you and four friends got stuck in an elevator and someone needed to call for help on the emergency phone, you**
    a. would have a hard time doing it.
    b. might not enjoy the task, but you would do it— it's an emergency!
    c. would volunteer to call.
    d. would call and make friends with the 911 operator.

11. **If a group of kids poked fun at your little brother, you would**
    a. come to life at the thought of having the opportunity to work a crowd.
    b. quietly explain that it is not okay to make fun of anyone.
    c. tell him to ignore them.
    d. use all your energy to teach those kids a life lesson.

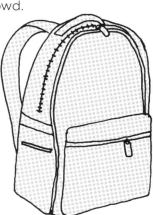

12. Your teacher is planning to assign four hours of homework the night before a test. You and your friends are outraged. It's too much work! You

   a. complain about the workload to your friends but then grin and bear it, because what else can you do?

   b. meet with your teacher in private to discuss whether it would be possible to make the homework assignment due at the end of the week.

   c. immediately raise your hand and protest.

   d. stew silently as you trudge through all the homework and studying that night.

13. If you had to be in charge of a group of people at a fair where you were volunteering, you would be

   a. uncomfortable.

   b. all right but exhausted after the event.

   c. exhilarated to be with such fun people.

   d. unstoppable and on top of your game.

14. If someone heard you singing in the shower, you would

    a. ask if she would like you to sing for her again.

    b. be so embarrassed, you would want to move away.

    c. expect compliments and feedback.

    d. be a little embarrassed.

15. Your ultimate birthday celebration would be

    a. a small family event at home.

    b. a block party that gets your whole neighborhood in on the celebration.

    c. a huge party at a restaurant.

    d. going to a movie and for ice cream with a few friends.

16. Which jobs are you most likely to pursue?

    a. Librarian, reporter

    b. Researcher, web designer

    c. Teacher, doctor, or nurse

    d. Singer, actress

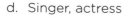

SCORECARD

Go over your answers and give yourself points according to the following chart:

1. a = 1, b = 3, c = 0, d = 2
2. a = 1, b = 3, c = 2, d = 0
3. a = 0, b = 3, c = 1, d = 2
4. a = 0, b = 3, c = 2, d = 1
5. a = 3, b = 1, c = 2, d = 0
6. a = 2, b = 0, c = 1, d = 3
7. a = 2, b = 3, c = 1, d = 0
8. a = 2, b = 0, c = 1, d = 3

9. a = 1, b = 0, c = 2, d = 3
10. a = 0, b = 1, c = 2, d = 3
11. a = 3, b = 1, c = 0, d = 2
12. a = 1, b = 2, c = 3, d = 0
13. a = 0, b = 1, c = 2, d = 3
14. a = 3, b = 0, c = 2, d = 1
15. a = 0, b = 3, c = 2, d = 1
16. a = 1, b = 0, c = 2, d = 3

0–11 Points: You're an Introvert

Sometimes you prefer the company of people, and sometimes you don't. After a social event, you may want to hang out solo for a while. You may also not enjoy speaking in front of a group of people. It's scary, but it could be something to work on!

12–24 Points: You're an Extroverted Introvert

You definitely like your "me time." That is okay because if you get enough time to unwind and chill by yourself, you love spending time with others!

25–36 Points: You're an Introverted Extrovert

Sometimes you like being by yourself, but mostly you like to have people all around you. They make you feel energized. You can be a little shy giving a presentation, but you get through it!

37–48 Points: You're an Extrovert You thrive on being with all kinds of personalities all the time. You rarely need your alone time, and maybe you love being the center of attention. Aside from when you are sleeping, you prefer to be in the mix.

TAKE ACTION

You can try being more extroverted or introverted to see what it's like. Play a game with yourself. The object of it is to lead the group. Let's say everyone wants to go to the park. See if you can persuade your group to take a walk instead. If everyone wants pizza for lunch, see if you can persuade everyone to have sandwiches. Then think about the experience. What skills did you need to change a person's mind? Did you enjoy the game?

Or are you the type of person who always talks the most in class or in a small group? Next time the teacher asks you a question, try giving someone else the chance to talk first even if you know the answer.

Think about the people in your life. How many of them are introverts? How many are extroverts? Make a chart. What can you say about the people who are introverts? What can you say about the people who are extroverts?

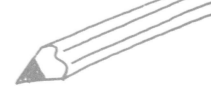

QUIZ 11

Some people seem to be born with money skills. They know how to earn, save, spend, and invest like champions. But it doesn't come that easily for everyone. If you've ever found yourself wondering "Where did my money go?" this quiz is for you! The good news is that it's never too late to improve your money skills. What's your smart money level? Let's find out.

1. **If you find a few bucks in your pocket, you**
    a. spend it immediately at the coffee shop or the drugstore.
    b. think about things you could buy for your jewelry-making business that would help you increase your profit.
    c. put it in your piggy bank.

2. **If money is tight, you can always**
    a. try to get a baby-sitting job.
    b. bring your lunch to school twice a week instead of buying it.
    c. ask a relative for a loan.

66

3. **If you are shopping for a new pair of jeans, what's your first priority?**
   a. The brand name
   b. The price
   c. The quality of the pants

4. **If you want a raise in allowance, you might tell your parents that you will**
   a. do a few extra chores around the house.
   b. cry if you don't get it.
   c. take on a new weekly chore such as unloading the dishwasher.

5. **You find that when you have to buy something with your own money, you are**
   a. less likely to buy it.
   b. not willing to spend your stash of cash.
   c. still going to buy it—you wouldn't buy something that wasn't worth it.

6. **What common saying about money do you most relate to?**
   a. Money doesn't grow on trees.
   b. Time is money.
   c Money burns a hole in your pocket.

7. **If you have a friend who always has a lot of cash, you**
   a. don't say no when she offers to pay for your candy at the movies.
   b. try not to let that bother you.
   c. remember that money is different for everyone.

8. **A great way to save money is to**
   a. buy only things that are on sale.
   b. swap things such as party dresses, books, and magazines.
   c. sew your own clothes.

9. **What do you need to know about setting up a lemonade stand?**

   a. You will have to spend money to make money.

   b. You can charge a lot of money for a small glass.

   c. You will need a good recipe for lemonade.

10. **Your best friend gave you a $25 gift card at your favorite store for your birthday. Now her birthday is coming up and you have only $20. What can you do?**

   a. Give her the $20 and make her something beautiful such as a poster, a photo of the two of us, or a plant.

   b. Ask a parent for the five bucks. Give the friend the same thing she got me, so that it's fair.

   c. Plan a special picnic day and make all her favorite foods.

11. **If you see a beaded bracelet in a store and fall in love with it, what do you do?**

   a. Call my mom and dad and ask them to meet me at the store with money.

   b. Buy one for myself and one for a friend.

   c. Think about if I really need that bracelet and if it will really make me happy.

12. **Why are banks important?**

   a. They provide people with jobs.

   b. They store our money in a safe place.

   c. They enable people and companies to borrow money.

13. **How do you feel about your attitude toward money?**

   a. I am always thinking about ways to make it.

   b. I worry I may be too uptight.

   c. I think that not having enough of it prevents me from having the things I want.

14. What do you think your money situation will be in fifteen years?

a. I will be independently wealthy.

b. I am hopeful that I will be able to make a good living doing a job I like.

c. I worry that I will never have enough money.

15. A good friend tells you that if you invest two months of allowance in a stock, he will triple your money. You

a. allow him to invest just one week's worth of your allowance.

b. talk to a parent or money mentor about it first.

c. let him have it because he's a good friend.

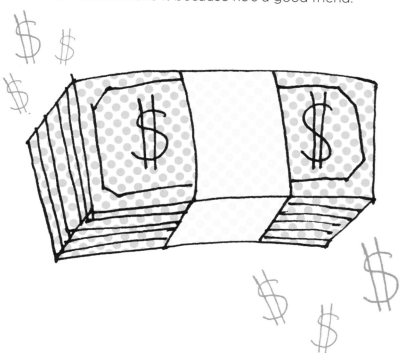

SCORECARD

Go over your answers and give yourself points according to the following chart:

1. a = 3, b = 2, c = 1
2. a = 1, b = 2, c = 3
3. a = 3, b = 1, c = 2
4. a = 2, b = 3, c = 1
5. a = 2, b = 3, c = 1
6. a = 1, b = 2, c = 3
7. a = 3, b = 2, c = 1
8. a = 3, b = 2, c = 1
9. a = 1, b = 3, c = 2
10. a = 2, b = 3, c = 1
11. a = 3, b = 2, c = 1
12. a = 3, b = 1, c = 2
13. a = 2, b = 1, c = 3
14. a = 3, b = 2, c = 1
15. a = 2, b = 1, c = 3

15–24 Points: Money Mogul

You've got great money skills! You value the money that you earn and are always looking for ways to make more. Talk to a parent or money manager about investing your money or starting your own business. And remember, sometimes it is okay to spend money on something you want or want to give to others.

25–35 Points: Average Money Skills

You're on the right track! Making decisions about money may make you a bit nervous, but don't worry too much. Follow the habits of a parent or relative who has a smart sense about money. Talk about your money challenges with that person frequently. After a while, you will develop money smarts of your own.

36–45 Points: In Need of Money Skills
You're not the best with money, but things can always turn around! Talk to someone whose money skills you admire and follow these tips to start being smarter about money right away:

- Fill a piggy bank with leftover change to save up for something useful.
- Make a budget and stick to it. Think about your actions before spending.
- Keep a list of all the items you buy in a month. Then review it and see which things were smart purchases and which ones were not so smart.

Once you see that you are in control of your money, you will gain more confidence in the money skills department.

TAKE ACTION

Pick two people you know personally or are familiar with from the media. If you know them personally, interview them about money. Ask them about their saving and spending habits. If a person is in the media, read up on how he or she became wealthy. What can you learn about money from other people?

Pets can be a lot of fun. You get to play with them and cuddle them, and it seems like they're always happy to see you. But they can also be a lot of responsibility—you have to make sure you're prepared to take care of your new pet. Are you ready to take that on? What type of pet might be best for you? Let's find out.

1. During the day at your house, a parent or caregiver is

    a. always home.

    b. usually not home.

    c. home most of the time.

    d. never home.

2. How would you describe your home life?

    a. There's a lot of drama but also lots of laughter.

    b. It's a madhouse.

    c. I have a medium-size family; things are kind of laid back and chill.

    d. It's quiet; I'm an only child.

3. Who would mostly be in charge of caring for the pet?

    a. My baby-sitter would be.

    b. Mom or Dad would be.

    c. We will all take turns.

    d. I would be.

4. How does everyone in your house feel about the idea of getting a pet?

    a. Excited

    b. Happy

    c. Overwhelmed

    d. Scared

5. Can you afford a pet?

    a. I think so?

    b. Yes!

    c. We've been saving for a while, and we've made a budget.

    d. Not really, but I do want one.

6. Have you or has anybody in your house had experience with a pet before?

    a. No, we've never dealt with any kind of animal before.

    b. No, but how hard can it be?

    c. At least one of my parents had pets while growing up.

    d. Yes, this is not my first pet.

7. Why do you want a pet?

    a. I want someone to take walks with and play fetch with.

    b. I just want one!

    c. I want something soft and furry to cuddle with.

    d. Lots of my friends have pets.

8. Which of the following sounds most doable to you?

   a. Playing with an animal when I want to but having someone else be the main caregiver

   b. Cleaning an animal cage or litter box and being in charge of two daily feedings

   c. Feeding a pet twice a day

   d. Walking an animal two to four times a day, feeding it twice, and playing with it for a little while each day

9. Is anyone in your family allergic to furry pets?

   a. My sister is, but we won't let the pet go in her room.

   b. I don't think so.

   c. I'm allergic, but I don't care!

   d. No—we've all had allergy tests.

10. How much time can you devote to your pet each day?

   a. All my time after school

   b. Maybe half an hour because I'm pretty busy

   c. A few minutes before I rush out the door to school

   d. I've got swim practice, but there are still two hours between that and bed.

11. How much space do you have for the pet?

   a. I could get rid of some of the stuffed animals on my bed.

   b. We have a small house, but there's a park nearby.

   c. We live in an apartment, but there's a courtyard.

   d. We have a big fenced-in yard.

12. True or false: I will not care about the pet hair all over my clothes and furniture.

    a. Hmm, all over my clothes?

    b. That's mostly true.

    c. That's very true.

    d. I don't like the sound of that.

13. True or false: I am always running, jumping, and playing, so having a pet that likes to move will be great.

    a. I like having a companion.

    b. That's somewhat true.

    c. I don't run or jump unless I am in gym class and I have to.

    d. That's very true.

14. If you and your family had to leave town for the weekend, how easy would it be to find a reliable person to watch your pet?

    a. I might be able to find a friend from school.

    b. My grandma can come by once a day.

    c. We'd have to board the pet somewhere.

    d. Our neighbor has already offered!

15. I am hoping that my future pet will be

    a. a friend who will always love me.

    b. something I can post pictures of on social media.

    c. my best buddy.

    d. something to cuddle with.

SCORECARD

Go over your answers and give yourself points according to the following chart:

1. a = 4, b = 2, c = 3, d = 1
2. a = 2, b = 1, c = 3, d = 4
3. a = 1, b = 2, c = 4, d = 3
4. a = 3, b = 4, c = 2, d = 1
5. a = 2, b = 4, c = 3, d = 1
6. a = 1, b = 2, c = 3, d = 4
7. a = 4, b = 1, c = 3, d = 2
8. a = 1, b = 3, c = 2, d = 4
9. a = 3, b = 2, c = 1, d = 4
10. a = 4, b = 2, c = 1, d = 3
11. a = 1, b = 3, c = 2, d = 4
12. a = 2, b = 3, c = 4, d = 1
13. a = 3, b = 2, c = 1, d = 4
14. a = 1, b = 2, c = 3, d = 4
15. a = 3, b = 1, c = 4, d = 2

15–26 Points: Not So Ready for a Pet

It's okay to appreciate animals from afar. If your life is busy or if your parents don't have the resources for a pet, try to appreciate your friends' pets. If having a pet is something you really want, try to plan for it in the next few years. Save some money, clear a space, and see if you can make room in your schedule. If you can't, take lots of day trips to the zoo—or try volunteering at the local animal shelter!

27–38 Points: Start with Something Small

It might be a good idea for you to try a pet that doesn't need a ton of attention. Have you thought about a fish, mouse, or rat? A turtle might be a good option for you, but keep in mind that a turtle does not interact with you.

A snake might be another option, but remember that although they are relatively easy—they eat only once a week, and they are clean and quiet—you will need to feed them mice on a weekly basis. Also, snakes can get sick and can bite.

39–49: Maybe Keep It to a Cat

You want the love and the responsibility of a pet, but you may not have the time or the space for a dog. A cat could be ideal. Cats are independent and don't need you to walk them. While some cats are aloof and don't require much stimulation from humans, others enjoy cuddling.

A guinea pig also could work. You will get the affection and love that a dog can offer but not the mess and the time commitment that a dog requires. Also, a guinea pig, unlike a hamster, keeps the same hours you do. It can be left alone, but guinea pigs like love and affection. In fact, prepare to hear vocal sounds whenever you enter the room. That's your guinea pig letting you know that it would like to play. These babies are soft and sweet, but you don't have to walk them around the block!

50–60 Points: Future Pet Owner

It sounds like you're ready for a pet! You could look into getting a dog, cat, ferret, or bird. You have the space, time, and support to keep a creature happy and healthy. If you do get a dog, try to match the breed to the amount of exercise you can give it. A pug doesn't need more than a brisk walk around the block daily, but a greyhound or a Lab will require a lot more movement than that. Enjoy your new friend, you animal lover!

TAKE ACTION

There are lots of animals that work for people. These animals, such as guide dogs, help people who cannot fully take care of themselves. Read up on animals that help people, and then share what you've learned with your friends. Is there any way you can become involved in the cause? Maybe there is a fund-raising or volunteer opportunity.

QUIZ 13

WHICH CHILDREN'S BOOK CHARACTER ARE YOU?

Have you ever read a story and felt that you connected with a character? Maybe he or she (or it!) was just as zany or friendly or adventurous as you are. Which character from a classic children's book are you?

Let's find out.

1. **If you were sent to your bedroom for misbehaving, you would spend the time**
    a. doodling—on the walls.
    b. writing rhyming poems.
    c. texting with your best friend.
    d. thinking of escaping from your room by building a secret tunnel in your closet.

2. **If guests were coming over for a party, you might serve**
    a. cookies, ice cream, and more ice cream.
    b. a tray of strange snacks, such as marshmallows and French-fried oysters or mushroom caps with crushed peppermint candy.
    c. a huge salad from your vegetable garden.
    d. soup and sandwiches.

3. Your feel most comfortable in flip-flops and

    a. a warm-up suit.

    b. a neon-colored onesie.

    c. faded jeans and a T-shirt.

    d. a camouflage-print cape and matching cap.

4. Your favorite day trip might be to

    a. the zoo.

    b. a carnival.

    c. a hay ride.

    d. the alligator races.

5. If you were writing a book about your life, it might be called

    a. *Lessons I've Learned Over and Over Again*.

    b. *Things That Only Happen to Me*.

    c. *My One True Friend*.

    d. *Journey to Another Land*.

6. What advice about life would you give to your younger sibling?

    a. Play all day and all night.

    b. Build robots and let them do all the work for you.

    c. Treat your friends fairly and with kindness.

    d. Get in touch with your animal side—roar!

7. Your favorite topic of conversation is

    a. what's going on with your friends.

    b. the business of cloning.

    c. how to make the planet greener.

    d. animal behavior.

8. What is your favorite thing to eat that's green?

    a. Green bananas

    b. Green tea with green tamales

    c. Salad and more salad

    d. Broccoli soup and a sandwich with greens

9. If you could follow your own advice, it would be to

    a. be quiet and listen.

    b. play lots of games.

    c. take a daily stroll with a friend.

    d. be brave!

10. When you're thirsty, you drink

    a. anything that is around.

    b. milk or ice-cold water with a colored straw.

    c. water from the pond.

    d. a mystery drink that will give you superpowers.

11. To you, the best thing about life is

    a. acting silly with friends.

    b. finding a path that no one else has ever explored.

    c. having a friend to share in all the fun.

    d. using your imagination.

12. Pick a future profession.

    a. A clown or stand-up comedian

    b. A digital artist or city planner

    c. A psychologist or teacher

    d. A theme park designer

13. If you invented a line of clothing, what would it be called?

    a. Monkey Business

    b. Over the Hill and Around the Bend

    c. Friends for Always

    d. Imagine That!

14. Who would you invite to a tea party?

    a. A man wearing a yellow hat

    b. Two strange children

    c. A pal

    d. Imaginary monsters

15. Your teachers say you are

    a. mischievous and funny.

    b. intelligent and great with words.

    c. a tender-hearted soul.

    d. an imaginative storyteller.

SCORECARD

Mostly A's: George from *Curious George* by H. A. Rey

You are eager and curious, and you love to be in the center of everything. You may be sweet and friendly, but you can also be a little too curious for your own good. Always listen to the man in the yellow hat!

Mostly B's: The Cat in the Hat from *The Cat in the Hat* by Dr. Seuss

Stylish, zany, and full of pizazz—that's you! You find clever ways to play with words, and you can build some amazingly fun contraptions. Oh, the places you will go!

Mostly C's: Frog or Toad from the *Frog and Toad* books by Arnold Lobel

Just like Frog and Toad, you are in a strong friendship and your best bud is very much a part of your life. In fact, you don't know where you'd be without that friend! You are always there to help to your friend, and he or she does the same for you. The simple pleasures in life are what's important to the two of you.

Mostly D's: Max from *Where the Wild Things Are* by Maurice Sendak

You, my friend, are highly imaginative. You know how to dream up some fun from the shelter of your own four walls. You can create characters and adventures that will entertain everyone. Keep the story alive! Just remember to try not to go to bed without your supper.

TAKE CHARGE

You may be too old for picture books, but remember how absolutely wonderful they are? Spend an afternoon in the young children's section of the library and revisit some of the greats. Don't you just love Madeline, Olivia, Pinkalicious, Henry and Mudge, and Winnie-the-Pooh?

QUIZ 14

WHAT'S YOUR DREAM JOB?

Have you thought about what you might like to do when you grow up? It's a long way away, but it can be interesting—and fun—to think about! Sometimes different types of people fit best in certain jobs. What job best suits you? Let's find out.

1. **How would your kindergarten teacher describe you?**
   a. Helpful
   b. Persuasive
   c. Creative
   d. Sweet
   e. Smart

2. **What is your favorite subject?**
   a. Science
   b. Social studies
   c. Art
   d. English
   e. Computer skills

3. If a friend needed help solving a family problem, what would you do?

   a. Give practical advice

   b. Present both sides of the argument so that your friend can see the whole picture

   c. Propose a new idea that may shed light on the problem

   d. Talk with your friend's family members so they feel better about the problem

   e. Research the problem online and share your findings with your friend

4. What kind of young child were you?

   a. Helpful

   b. Stubborn

   c. Brilliant

   d. Social

   e. Great at computers

5. What's most important to you in your life?

   a. Solving problems

   b. Standing up for what you believe in

   c. Creating something important

   d. Getting along with others

   e. Figuring out why

6. If money was no object and you never had to work, what would you do?

   a. Work to find a cure for cancer

   b. Work to promote justice

   c. Paint, sing, write, take pictures

   d. Volunteer as a tutor

   e. Play video games all day

7. Where would you most like to volunteer?

a. A hospital
b. A newspaper office
c. A graphic design firm
d. A summer camp
e. A tech start-up

8. What's a hobby that appeals to you?

a. Running
b. Working with a local campaign
c. Playing with Legos
d. Hosting a book group
e. Playing computer games

9. What do you see yourself wearing to work?

a. A uniform
b. A business dress
c. Casual clothes
d. Nice but comfortable outfits
e. Jeans

10. On a free Saturday you might

a. take a yoga class.
b. go to a movie.
c. check out a new museum.
d. have a party with friends.
e. start building your own computer.

11. What part of the newspaper appeals most to you?

a. The health section
b. The big headlines
c. The entertainment section
d The advice column
e. Tech news and stocks

12. What's your job at a party?

   a. Making guests feel comfortable
   b. Leading a discussion about current events
   c. Manning the chocolate fountain
   d. Making sure to talk to everyone
   e. Creating an awesome playlist

13. What type of TV show are you most into?

   a. A medical drama
   b. Anything set in Washington, D.C.
   c. A documentary about creative inventions
   d. An emotional family drama
   e. A show about computer hackers

14. When you think of yourself at work, you see yourself

   a. in an office.
   b. all over the place.
   c. both inside and outside.
   d. It doesn't matter as long as you are with people.
   e. it doesn't matter as long as you have your computer.

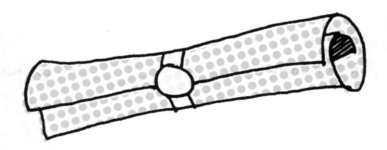

SCORECARD

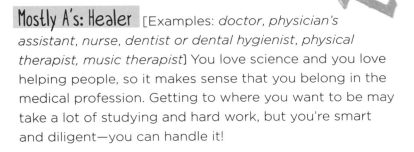

Mostly A's: Healer
[Examples: *doctor, physician's assistant, nurse, dentist or dental hygienist, physical therapist, music therapist*] You love science and you love helping people, so it makes sense that you belong in the medical profession. Getting to where you want to be may take a lot of studying and hard work, but you're smart and diligent—you can handle it!

Mostly B's: Defender of the Law
[Examples: *police officer, parole officer, lawyer, judge, paralegal, politician, political writer, speechwriter, history professor*] You have strong feelings about the way life should work: You follow the rules, do the right thing, and expect others to do the same. The government and its laws interest you greatly, and you can't wait to learn more about them!

Mostly C's: Creator
[Examples: *actor, director, singer, musician, dancer, visual artist, designer, writer, architect, builder, city planner*] Artsy and creative, you are an inventor. Your interest in the arts—dance, theater, music, fine art—may turn into an amazing career. Or maybe you'll put your imagination to use by designing buildings or cities!

Mostly D's: People Person [Examples: *teacher*, *mentor*, *psychologist*, *therapist*, *moderator*, *human resources manager*]

You are gifted when it comes to helping people understand or overcome hardships. Your empowering personality will serve you well in a career working with others to teach them things or try to fix their problems. When two friends fight, you're great at sorting things out, which could make you a wonderful moderator—a person who helps keep emotions at bay when people are going through difficult things, such as a divorce.

Mostly E's: Computer Whiz [Examples: *web designer*, *coder*, *database engineer*, *information technology manager*, *programmer*]

Is there anything you can't do with a computer? You can design web pages, write code, engineer databases, and program computers. You are all about the information age. Who knows? Right now you may even be creating your own robot.

TAKE ACTION

Start talking now with your friends and family about their jobs. When you meet someone who has a job that interests you, see if you can sit down and talk to him or her about it. Maybe you can visit the person on the job to gain a sense of what his or her day is like.

QUIZ 15

WHAT SEASON ARE YOU?

Did you ever wonder which season makes you happiest? Are you the first one to dive into the water during summer? Do you absolutely love spending time in a pumpkin patch in fall? Is winter your favorite time when all you need is a snowman and some snow pants? Or does spring, with its flowers and chirping birds, make you smile the most?

Let's find out.

1.   You're dressing up for a school concert today. Your outfit is jeans and a(n) _____ top.
   a.   white
   b.   orange
   c.   gray
   d.   pink

2.   Which scene sounds most appealing to you?
   a.   A huge party
   b.   A walk in the woods
   c.   A night on the couch watching movies
   d.   A game in the park

3. Your friends are over. What's the perfect snack for you guys?

    a. A bowl of cherries

    b. Apples and caramel dip

    c. Brownies

    d. Chips and salsa

4. You would be lost without your

    a flip-flops.

    b. gray hoodie.

    c. favorite scarf.

    d. jean jacket.

5. What's your favorite holiday?

    a. July 4

    b. Halloween

    c. Valentine's Day

    d. Earth Day

6. Your favorite sport is

    a. volleyball.

    b. football.

    c. basketball.

    d. lacrosse.

7. If you had personalized stationery, with what would it be decorated?

    a. Sprinkles

    b. Ribbons

    c. Stars

    d. Flowers

8. You love walks. When you go on them, you make sure you always have your
- a. water bottle.
- b. walking boots.
- c. gloves.
- d. phone to take pics.

9. On your next family vacation, you hope to
- a. go on an African safari.
- b. visit Vermont.
- c. go on an Alaskan cruise.
- d. take a trip to London.

10. On your neck, you'd love to wear a chain with a(n)
- a. ruby.
- b. topaz.
- c. amethyst.
- d. emerald.

11. Your favorite part of the Thanksgiving meal is
- a. cranberry dressing.
- b. pumpkin pie.
- c. mashed potatoes.
- d. turkey.

12. What's your favorite place to see a movie?
- a. At the drive-in
- b. Movie night in the park on a blanket
- c. In your living room
- d. At the movie theater

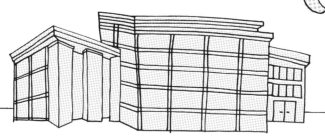

93

SCORECARD

Mostly A's: Summer You are fun, laid back, and cheerful—just like summer! Summer means no school, warm weather, and lots of downtime to chill. And when it gets too hot, you are more than happy to make a splash by jumping in the water.

Mostly B's: Fall You are confident and comfortable in your own skin. You love to admire nature. Take advantage of the fall season by getting out there and picking apples, taking hayrides, and living life to the fullest.

Mostly C's: Winter You are strong-willed and dependable. In addition to loving winter sports, winter days, and winter holidays, you pride yourself on the fact that you know how to weather a storm.

Mostly D's: Spring You are thoughtful and kind, and you love floral prints almost as much as you love sitting in your garden planting flowers. The spring is a time when you look forward to rejuvenation. You might try a whole new look around this time of year.

TAKE ACTION

Brainstorm a list of things you like about every season. Then make a list of things that you would like to do in each of the four seasons. Save your list, and try to do everything on it before you reach the ripe age of twenty.

HAPPY QUIZZING!

The most important thing about personality quizzes is to remember that they're just for fun! There are no wrong answers. Take the quizzes to get to know your friends, get to know yourself, and learn about the world. You can even try making up your own!

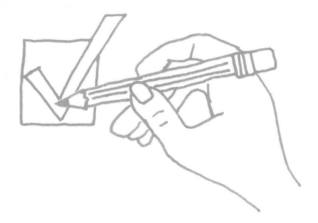